Terrance Talks Travel:
The Quirky Tourist Guide to Kathmandu
(Nepal) & The Himalayas

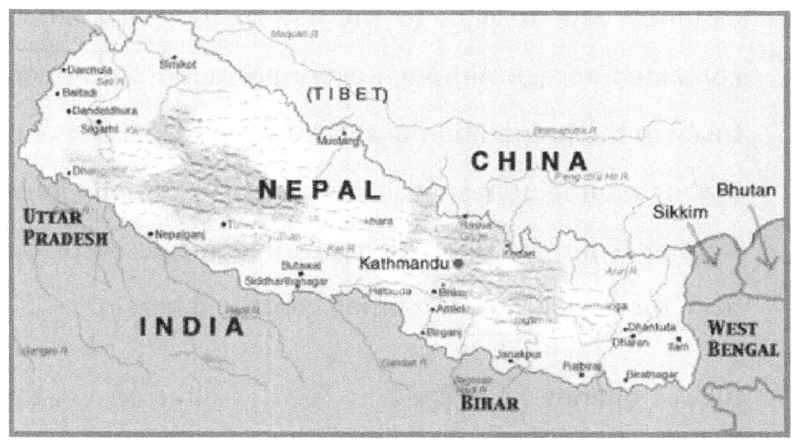

Terrance Zepke

TERRANCE TALKS TRAVEL: The Quirky Tourist Guide to Kathmandu (Nepal) | Terrance Zepke

Copyright © 2018 by Terrance Zepke

All queries should be directed to: www.safaripublishing.net.

For more about the author, www.terrancezepke.com and www.terrancetalkstravel.com.

TERRANCE TALKS TRAVEL: The Quirky Tourist Guide to Kathmandu (Nepal) | Terrance Zepke

Library of Congress Cataloging-in-Publication Data

ISBN: 9781942738503

America/Zepke, Terrance p.cm.

Terrance Talks Travel: The Quirky Tourist Guide to Kathmandu (Nepal)

1. Travel-Nepal. 2. Adventure Travel-Asia. 3. Kathmandu. 4. Himalaya Mountains-Great Himalayan Trail. 5. Nepal. 6. Kathmandu guidebook. 7. Asia-Travel. 8. Chitwan National Park. 9. Mount Everest trekking. 10. Temples-Asia. 11. Nepal guidebook. 12. Mountaineering-mountain climbing. 13. Nepal wildlife. 14. Nonfiction-spiritual. I. Title.

First edition

Safari Publishing

CONTENTS

INTRODUCTION

The average tourist goes sightseeing. The quirky tourist *travels*. He immerses himself in the local culture. He seeks out weird attractions, offbeat destinations, and adventurous activities. He tries new things, meets lots of people, and has a lot of fun along the way.

There aren't many places quirkier than Kathmandu. Not only is this capital city full of ancient and amazing temples, exciting activities like mountain flights and extreme zip flying, and a dazzling Himalayan backdrop, it is a melting pot of dozens of ethnic groups across three kingdoms (Kathmandu, Bhaktapur, and Patan). Since Kathmandu is the gateway to the Himalayas, expect to encounter some wild and crazy trekkers along the way. Nepalese cuisine is an adventure in and of itself with unusual dishes like jellied yak meat, bamboo shoot soup, and butter tea. Enjoy a glass of wine made at the world's highest altitude vineyard, or try Raksi, a strong drink comparable to sake, which is produced at rustic distilleries and is *not* aged before distribution. Adventurous travelers can sip or slurp specialty cocktails, including the Everest Cooler and the Annapurna Special.

Nepal offers tourists tea house trekking, massive mountain ranges that include the world's highest mountain ranges, Mt. Everest and Annapurna; the Forbidden Kingdom of Mustang, Buddhist monastery tours, meditation retreats, Hindu festivals, remote refuges and sanctuaries filled with rare wildlife like the Royal Bengal Tiger, Red Panda, and Greater One-horned Rhino; and so much more!

Quirky travelers will delight in all the adventure options offered, such as the world's highest whitewater rafting, bungee jumping off Bhote Kosi River Bridge, paragliding over Phewa Tal, thrilling Everest Flights, elephant polo games, elephant-back safaris, bicycling across the Kathmandu Valley, trekking, and mountaineering. But forget trying to learn the native language because more than 100 languages are spoken!

Nepal is one of my favorite places because it has so much to see and do—the perfect place for an adventure traveler. You won't fit it all in unless you have several weeks, so you need to plan carefully, especially if you want to do some trekking too. Also, there are lots of religious and social taboos, as you can imagine. I share many tips and caveats throughout this reference so you won't accidentally offend anyone during your stay.

Kathmandu offers an amazing array of lodging, dining, and nightlife that range from budget to luxury and laid back to frenetic. In addition to being a place filled with spiritual enlightenment and adventure, Nepal is also a great place for budget travelers. Suitable accommodations can be obtained for just a few bucks a night or you can upgrade to "deluxe" for just a few dollars more. Food is also quite cheap, so you can try many new things for minimal cost. Souvenirs are a bargain if you go to the right places. Admission fees are usually nominal. Best of all, it is a safe place to visit with highly hospitable locals who warmly welcome travelers who dare to venture all the way to the "Rooftop of the World." Those who do will find the journey was well worth it.

So read on and get ready for what might be your biggest and best adventure ever.

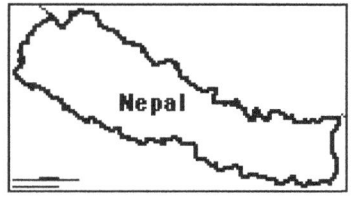

FYI: Despite the entire country of Nepal being roughly the same size as the U.S. state, Arkansas, its population is more than 29 million (whereas the population Arkansas is less than three million).

GETTING THERE

Nepal is a land-locked country with Tibet and
China to its north, India to its south, east, and
west. Bhutan and Bangladesh are close
neighbors. Many travelers will enter Nepal
overland from India by vehicle or train or fly
from Delhi to Kathmandu.
(http://www.indianrail.gov.in/enquiry/StaticPage
s/StaticEnquiry.jsp?StaticPage=index.html). If
you travel by train, you will have to take a bus
for the last leg of the trip. Or you can take a
direct bus from Delhi to Kathmandu
(http://www.delhi.gov.in/wps/wcm/connect/DOI
T_DTC/dtc/all+services/delhi-
kathmandu+bus+service). Or you can travel with
a tour group and leave the logistics to your
guide. This is a long journey if you don't fly, or

a ninety-minute flight on Air India or Nepal
Airlines, which is the national airline
(http://www.nepalairlines.com.np/home). It is
challenging to enter Nepal overland from China
because you have to pass through Tibet, which
has *many* travel restrictions and documents. It is
impossible to enter from Bhutan unless you are
part of a tour group. The only feasible overland
solution is India.

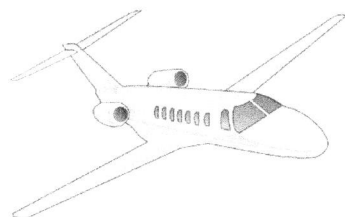

By Air

Most tourists will arrive at Tribhuvan
International Airport. More than thirty
international airlines fly into Kathmandu,
including Cathay Pacific, Air Asia, Air Arabia,
Thai Airways, Nepal Airlines, Jet Airways,

Virgin Atlantic, United Airlines, Lufthansa, Air India, Turkish Airlines, Korean Air, Singapore Airlines, Qatar Airways, Oman Air, China Southern, Air China, Emirates, British Airways, and Etihad Airways. http://www.tiairport.com.np/ and

https://www.nepalairflight.com/nepal_airlines/

Note: If you would like help booking your flights, **Nepal Travels** is a U.S., Canada, and Nepal-based full-service travel agency serving the travel needs of American, Canadian, Nepali, and other travelers around the world. Their Kathmandu office is staffed with experienced travel professionals and is open 24/7 for your convenience.
http://www.nepaltravelsonline.com/

Documentation: All tourists are required to have a passport to enter the country. Visas are required for most tourists. To obtain a tourist visa, apply for a visa at a Nepalese embassy or consulate before traveling, or purchase a tourist visa upon arrival at Kathmandu's Tribhuvan International Airport (www.tiairport.com.np). Please note that some nationals must obtain a tourist visa before arrival.

http://us.nepalembassy.gov.np/visa/

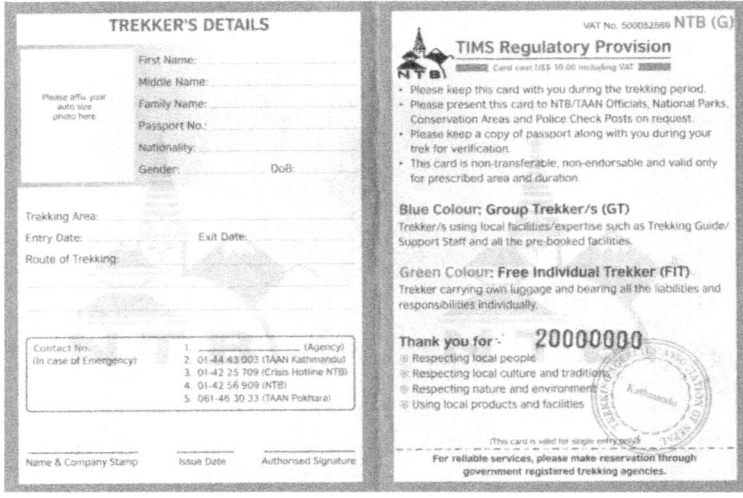

Trekking: You'll also need a trekking permit if you plan to go into restricted areas. For more information please check with Nepal immigration office, www.nepalimmigration.gov.np/content/trekking -permit-fees.html. Additionally, all trekkers are required to have a TIMS (Trekkers' Information Management Systems) Card. You will need a copy of your passport, two passport size photos, your travel insurance policy information, and applicable fees. While proof of travel insurance is not required, it is advisable to obtain a policy in case you have a medical emergency. Applications are made at the Trekking Agencies' Association Nepal (TAAN) Office in Maligaon, TIMS Counter at the Nepal Tourist Center in Kathmandu on Pradarshani Marg (open seven days week including holidays), and Government registered trekking companies in Kathmandu and Pokhara. The fee varies according to the trekking route and number of persons trekking. https://www.welcomenepal.com/plan-your-trip/tims-card.html. To find out fees for specific treks, http://www.taan.org.np/pages/trekking-permit-fees. If you'd like to do a guided trek, which I highly advise, you may find guides in

Kathmandu. Also, here is a reputable operator:
https://www.visithimalayastrek.com/.

FYI: Before you apply for a TIMS card in Kathmandu, you need to know: Trekking entry and exit dates (can be best estimate), Trekking entry and exit points, Trekking route/itinerary, Emergency contact info for Nepal (can use a tour agency as a contact), and Emergency contact info for someone in your home country. Also, you have to pay in Nepalese rupees. There is an ATM outside the tourist office.

Getting Around Kathmandu

By Taxi: You won't have to even search for one. You'll be asked if you need a ride before you even start looking. Just be sure to use a metered taxi or agree on the price before you get in the vehicle. One caveat, many cab drivers will

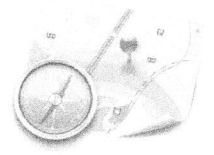

not use their meters unless you demand it before you set out. Be firm with your instructions and tell them "no" if they try to stop at a shop or attraction, unless you want to stop. Tips are not expected!

Nepal's answer to Uber: In Kathmandu there is a new motorbike ride-hailing app. **Tootle** (https://tootle.today) offers a cheaper and faster alternative to taxis, although the service is only offered until 8pm.

**F YI: The Kathmandu Tourist Center
provides free area maps and assistance for
travelers.**

**Public
Transportation:** There are public buses, as well
as tourist bus service to go into the valley or to
Chitwan and other popular tourist destinations.
Information on these options is available at the
Kathmandu Tourist Center.

Car rentals: **Green Path Transfers** offers
affordable and environmentally-friendly airport
transfers.
https://www.greenpathtransfers.com/destination/
kathmandu-airport-transfers

Trains: There is limited rail service in Nepal.

http://www.nepal.com/train-stations/

 **Other modes of**

transportation: Bicycles, scooters, and

mountain bikes can be rented. Also, e-rickshaws

can be hired.

For more tourism info,

https://www.welcomenepal.com/

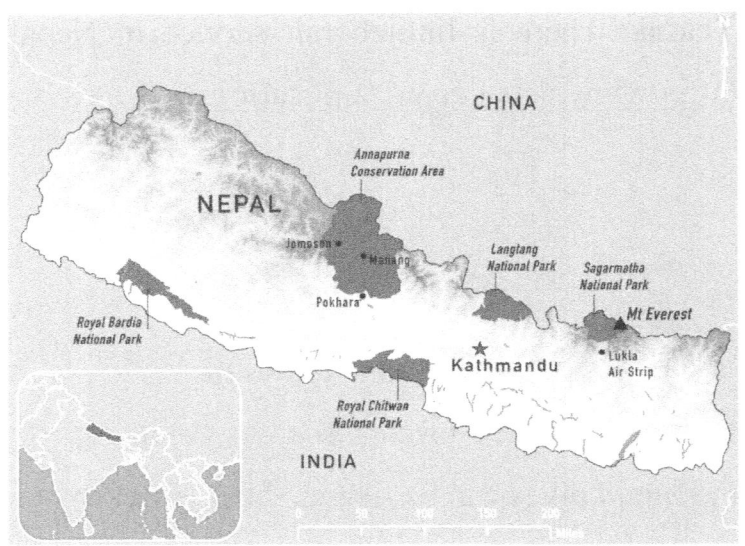

Fast Facts

Country Size: 56,827 square miles or 147,181 km²
(roughly the same size as Arkansas); Kathmandu is less
than twenty square miles (50km).

Capital: Kathmandu

Median age: 22

Population: 29 million (1.5 million Kathmandu + 3
million across Kathmandu Valley)

Currency: Nepalese Rupee

Culture: Nepalese culture is quite different from Western
cultures. The people are friendly but conservative.
Always ask before you enter take someone's photograph
or enter their premises.

Official Language: Nepali but 22 major languages are
recognized among Nepal's nearly three dozen different
ethnic groups. English is widely spoken and understood
in Kathmandu valley.

Time Zone: Nepal Standard Time (NPT) is the time zone
for Nepal. With a time offset from Coordinated Universal
Time (UTC) of +5:45 Greenwich Mean Time, it is one of
only three time zones with a 45-minute offset from UTC.

Electricity: 220V, 5H. Most of the power in Nepal comes
from hydro-power, which is not very reliable.

Nickname: Rooftop of the World

Leading Exports: Beverages and spirits, textiles, coffee,
tea, spices, and footwear. Tourism is becoming
increasingly important. Nearly one million tourists visited
Nepal last year.

Mountain climbing: Nepal is one of the best places to go in the world since it has eight of the world's fourteen highest mountains, including Mount Everest. The Great Himalayan Trail extends 2,800 miles.

Seasons: Nepal has four seasons: autumn, winter, spring, summer (also known as monsoon season).

IMPORTANT INFORMATION!

FYI: Cash machines are widely found in the major tourist areas such as Pokhara and Kathmandu. But many of these charge high withdrawal (transaction) fees, so it's advisable to avoid small ATM transactions and get out a large amount of cash at one time – just make sure you hide it well.

**Try to use ATMs that have security guards or
look like they are in telephone boxes. It's not
because Kathmandu is unsafe, but it is always
best to avoid the attention of pickpockets,
which are worldwide and notoriously prey on
tourists.**

**If you need to transfer money internationally,
use Transferwise
(https://transferwise.com/us/), it's the fastest
and cheapest way to move money around
when travelling.**

**You will not find ATMs in rural areas, so
have enough cash and keep it secure (like in a
money belt under your shirt) if you travel
outside of Kathmandu.**

Flag of Federal Democratic Republic of Nepal

**FYI: The national flag of Nepal is the world's only
non-quadrilateral national flag. A combination of two
red pennants with a large blue border: the smaller
upper triangle is the rising sun on a horizontal
crescent moon and the lower triangle displays a white
twelve-pointed sun.**

Best Time to Visit: It depends on what you
want to do, such as trekking or sightseeing. The
seasons are fall, winter, spring, and summer
(a.k.a. monsoon season). **September -
November** is the best time for tourists to visit
Nepal as the skies are generally clear and the
views spectacular. Also, **March - April** is a
good time. For more on the weather, see the
'Annual Events & Average Temps' chapter and
'About Trekking' for more on the best time to
go and what you need to know.

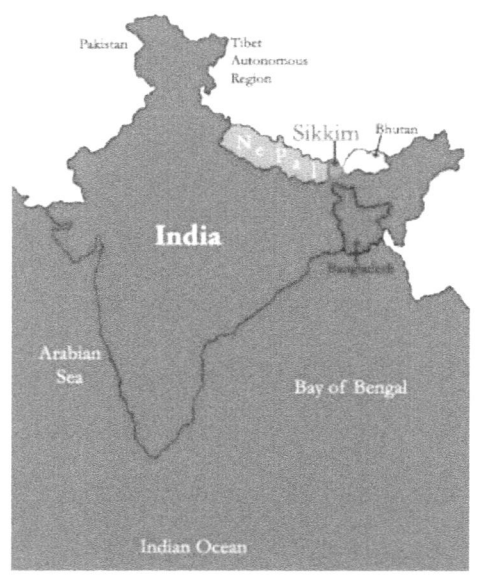

Although on some maps it appears that Nepal is bordered by Bhutan and Bangladesh, this is not true. A sliver of India separates Nepal from Bangladesh and Bhutan. Also, Tibet is part of China and Sikkum is an Indian state. So, to be correct, Nepal is bordered to the north by China and to the south, east, and west by India.

The Himalaya mountain system stretches across Nepal, Bhutan, Tibet, Afghanistan, China, and Pakistan. Himalaya literally means "Abode of Snow."

TERRANCE'S TOP TEN PICKS

1. **Trek to Mount Everest Base Camp.** This is the next best thing to climbing Mount Everest (29,029 feet) and is no small feat. Most of these treks depart from Kathmandu and fly into Lukla (highest airport in the world), so the

trek begins at nearly 7,900 feet into the village of Phakding. The next stop is Namche Bazaar, which is 10,000 feet. The trek takes about twelve days including acclimatization time to minimize altitude sickness.

More information on trekking can be found in the 'Adventure Activities' chapter. The Himalayas are home to 15,000 glaciers, three of the world's most

important river systems, jungles, medicinal herbs, and exotic animals. In fact, the Himalayas are home to 9% of the world's birds (850 species!) and 4% of mammal species, such as Bengal Tigers, Clouded Leopards, One-horned Rhinos, Snow Leopards, Himalayan Tahrs, and Blue Sheep.

Highlights: Besides the major achievement of reaching the base of Mount Everest (18,000 feet! Did you know that most wildlife does not venture above 20,000 and plant life is almost non-existnt), you may see rare wildlife, visit Tengboche Monastery, see remote villages and meet villagers, explore Sargamantha National Park, and learn about the Sherpa culture. More information about this trek is shared later in this reference.

Tengboche Monastery is one of the most renowned Buddhist monasteries in Nepal.

Rare Snow Leopard & Red Pandas

2. Wildlife watching. Nepal boasts more than
185 species of mammals, many of which cannot
be found anywhere else. Many are exotic and
rare, such as the Royal Bengal Tiger, Greater
One-Horned Rhino, Arna, Red Panda, and
Himalayan Snow Leopard. You may also see the
Asian Elephant, Tibetan Yak, Blue Sheep,
Himalayan Tahr, Langur, Sloth Bear, Chital,
Barking Deer, Blackbuck, and Swamp Deer. I
know it's hard to believe but there are otters and
dolphins in Nepal. Nepal has more than 850
species of birds and more than half of these can
be found in Kathmandu Valley. Nepal is home to
nine percent of the world's bird species.

Other places to find wildlife include
Chitwan National Park, which is a 6.5 hour
drive or short flight from Kathmandu to
Bharatpur. Chitwan was the first national park of

Nepal and is also a UNESCO World Heritage
Site. Reasonably-priced lodging includes
Chitwan Forest Resort, Chitwan Tiger Camp,
Wildlife Adventure Resort, and Jungle Wildlife
Camp. Deluxe lodging includes Tigerland Safari
Resort, Tiger Tops Tharu Lodge, Pugdungee
Safaris Barahi Jungle Lodge, and Tiger Tops
Elephant Camp. **Bardiya National Park** is
Nepal's largest park and it is also the most
remote. The park features nearly 68 species of
mammals and 544 bird species. Reptiles include
Gharial Crocodiles, Marsh-mugger Crocodiles,
and Gangetic Dolphins. Lodging is cheap,
including Mango Tree Lodge, Bardia Wildlife
Planet, Nature Safari Reserve Lodge, Jungle Base
Camp, and Rhino Lodge Bardia. The only deluxe
lodging is Tiger Tops Karnali Lodge.
Sagarmatha National Park is home of the

highest mountain peak in the world, Mt. Everest. One of the highest parks in the world, Sagarmatha was declared a UNESCO World Heritage Site in 1979. Wildlife is harder to spot here due to the terrain and the shyness of these animals, but trekkers may glimpse rare birds, Himalayan Black Bears, Himalayan Wolves, Ghorals, Serows, Red Pandas, Himalayan Snow Leopards, and the Himalayan Tahr—and the flora and fauna is spectacular. Due to the park's location, lodging options are fewer and pricier. The best bargains are Namche Hilltop Lodge and Restaurant and Himalayan Lodge. If you're looking for a higher caliber of lodging, there's Yeti Mountain Home Phakding, Yeti Mountain Home Namche, and Everest Summit Lodge Pargboche.

 **FYI: Nearly 6,000 flowering plant species grow in Nepal, including two percent of the world's orchids and six percent of the world's rhododendron species, which is Nepal's national flower.**

There are 250 plant species endemic to Nepal, which is why Nepal has earned the nickname, "<u>The Amazon of Asia</u>." Nepal is also home to over 650 different species of butterflies, as well as 850+ species of birds. So during your visit you will see many plants, birds,

butterflies, mammals, and reptiles that you will not find anywhere else in the world.

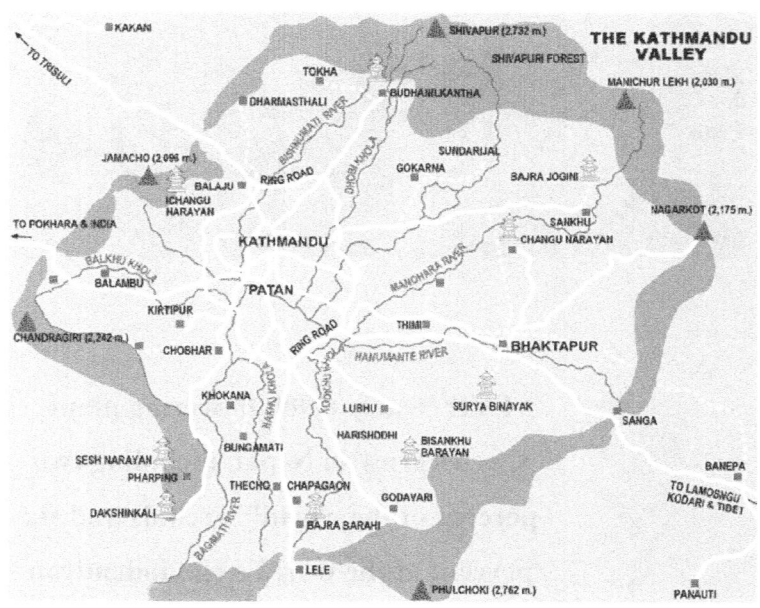

3. Explore Kathmandu Valley. The Kathmandu Valley is the most developed and populated place in Nepal. Kathmandu Valley includes three cities or "kingdoms" as they are often referred to—Kathmandu, Patan, and Bhaktapur. These were once independent

states ruled by the Malla kings. Today, the
Kathmandu Valley is home to seven world
heritage sites (Bhaktapur Durbar Square,
Changu Narayan Temple, Pashupatinath
Temple, Boudhanath Stupa, Kathmandu
Durbar Square, Swayambhunath Temple, and
Patan Durbar Square), which makes the entire
valley a UNESCO Cultural World Heritage
Site. Additionally, the valley is home to
hundreds of other ancient monuments,
sculptures, statues, stupas, and temples. The
Kathmandu Valley is a melting pot for
different cultures and religions. There are
numerous options, such as ox cart village
tours, cultural tours, general sightseeing,
attending one of Nepal's many festivals,
shopping for local handicrafts, full moon
concerts, night walking tours, and bicycle

tours across the valley. Be sure to admire architectural details, such as this window or the statues that line the entrance of this Bhaktapur.

FYI: Nepal is the only country with altitude variations ranging from 194 feet – 29,035 feet (59 meters - 8848 meters). Nepal has the highest lake (Tilicho) on the earth, the highest valley on earth (Arun Valley), the deepest gorge in Kaligandaki, the tallest grassland in the world in Chitwan National Park, and the densest concentration of world heritage site.

Look at this intricately designed window
on a Kathmandu house. Wow! It is known
as Desu Maru Jhya, which means "only
window of its kind."

Aren't these statues stunning? Such amazing
architecture and attention to detail can be found
all over the Kathmandu Valley, such as the Palace
of 55 Windows (Bhaktapur).

4. See the Living Goddess "Kumari". Kumari is derived from the Sanskrit word *Kaumarya*, which means princess. The tradition of worshipping a little girl (The princess must be pre-pubescent to ensure purity and chastity.) as a goddess dates back to the 17th century and is practiced by two of the world's oldest religions— Hinduism and Buddhism (Nepali Buddhists, not Tibetan Buddhists). The selection process is rigorous and it is considered to be a huge honor to be selected. In late August or early September, the annual Indra Jatra Festival is held. This is when Kumari is paraded all over Kathmandu. The girl is heavily made up with exotic eye makeup and garbed in elaborate ceremonial attire. She rides aboard something akin to a chariot while accompanied by masked men, which are part of her parade. There is dancing, music, and a big celebration during this festival celebrating the Living Goddess. This is the only chance to glimpse the Living Goddess. While there are several Kumaris throughout Nepal, the best known is the Royal Kumari of Kathmandu, and she lives in the Kumari Ghar, a palace in the center of the city.

**FYI: There are several legends telling of how the
current tradition of the Kumari began. According to
the most popular legend, a red serpent approached
the King Malla's chambers late one night as he
played tripasa, a dice game, with the goddess Taleju.
The goddess came along every night to play the game,
with the condition that the king refrain from telling
anyone about their meetings. But one night the king's
wife followed him to his chamber to find out who the
king was meeting so often. The king's wife saw
Taleju, which angered the goddess. She told the king
that if he wanted to see her again or have her protect
his country, he'd have to search for her among the
Newari (Shakya) community of Ratnawali, as she
would be incarnated as a little girl among them.
Hoping to make amends, King Jayaprakash Malla
left the palace in search of the young girl who was
possessed by Taleju's spirit.**

**Similarly, there is another story about the
disappearance of Taleju. The goddess visited King
Malla every night in the flesh. The king and the**

goddess played tripasa while discussing the country's
welfare. But one night the king made sexual advances
towards the goddess. As a result, she stopped visiting
the palace. The king pleaded for her return. Finally,
the goddess agreed to appear in the body of the virgin
girl from the Shakya family.

Even today, a mother's dream of a red serpent is
believed to be a portent of the elevation of her
daughter to the position of Royal Kumari. And each
year, the Nepalese King seeks the blessing of the
Royal Kumari at the festival of Indra Jatra.

**5. Experience a daily or annual ritual at
Pashupatinath Temple**, the oldest Hindu
temple in Kathmandu and a world heritage site.
Pashupatinath is also one of the very few living
cultural heritage sites in the world. The most
important rituals are the Maha Shiva Ratri Bala
Chaturthi Festival and Teej festival. During
these festivals, people from all over the world
come to worship. Hindu cremations are
performed here. Daily rituals include Morning

prayers, Farmayishi Puja, and Evening Aarati. Daily rituals at Pashupatinath are carried out by two sets of priests; Bhatt priests and Bhandari priests. Bhatt priests perform the daily ritual and can touch the lingam (idol), whereas Bhandari priests are temple caretaker priests who are not qualified to perform pooja (puja) rituals or even to touch the deity. Visitors are allowed restricted entry daily. The Evening Aarati is done by the shores of Bagmati and is very popular, so expect large crowds.

6. Get enlightened or at least a workout.
Swayambhunath Temple is the Sacred Buddhist
home of spiritual monkeys. This is a workout,
wildlife excursion, and spiritual escape all in

one! The workout is climbing the 365 steps into the temple. The wildlife includes hundreds of monkeys. The monkeys are considered holy to Tibetan Buddhists and Hindus. According to legend, Manjushree, the bodhisattva of wisdom, was in the process of raising the temple hill when the lice in his hair transformed into these monkeys. Swayambhunath means self-arisen and is derived from that legend. Located atop a hill west of Kathmandu city, the Swayambhunath complex has been in use since the 5th century A.D., so it is among the oldest religious sites in Nepal. It consists of a grand domed stupa and many shrines and temples. The stupa has Buddha's eyes and eyebrows painted onto it. Between them, the number one (in Devanagari script) is painted in the fashion of a nose. Each temple is ornate and decorated with

colorful prayer flags. A Tibetan monastery,
museum, and library are more recent additions.
In addition to the spiritual reward, visitors will
be rewarded with a panorama view of
Kathmandu Valley. The monkeys are most
active in the evenings, but they seem pretty
active to me all the time.

**FYI: The Symbolism of Swayambhunath…The dome
at the base represents the entire world. When a
person awakes (represented by eyes of wisdom and**

compassion) from the bonds of the world, the person reaches the state of enlightenment. The thirteen pinnacles on the top symbolize that sentient beings have to go through the thirteen stages of spiritual realizations to reach enlightenment or Buddhahood. There is a large pair of eyes on each of the four sides of the main stupa which represent Wisdom and Compassion. Above each pair of eyes is another eye, the third eye. It is said that when Buddha preaches, cosmic rays emanate from the third eye which acts as messages to heavenly beings so that those interested can come down to earth to listen to the Buddha.

Between the two eyes (also called Wisdom Eyes), a curly symbol, symbolizing the nose, is depicted which looks like a question mark, which is a Nepali sign of number figure one. This represents the unity of all things existing in the world as well as the only path to enlightenment through the teachings of Buddha.

There are carvings of the Panch Buddhas (five Buddhas) on each of the four sides of the stupa. There are also statues of the Buddhas at the base of

**the stupas. Each morning before dawn hundreds of
Buddhist (Vajrayana) and Hindu pilgrims ascend the
steps from the eastern side that lead up the hill,
passing the gilded Vajra (Tibetan: Dorje) and two
lions guarding the entrance, and begin a series of
clockwise circumambulations of the stupa.**

**7. Watch the World Elephant Polo
Championships.** Since 1982, Tiger Tops has
been hosting the World Elephant Polo
Championships in Nepal. The game consists of
the basic polo guidelines with a few necessary
changes to accommodate the size of the player's
mounts—a 6-10 ft. cane with a standard mallet
head on the end and each elephant carries two
riders who must rely on a mahout (who is an
elephant's trainer) to do the steering as they
shout out directions.

The rules are also a bit different. An elephant who lies down in front of the goal mouth will receive a foul. If they use their trunk to pick up the ball, that is a foul and earns their opponent a free hit. Half-time snacks include fresh cut grass and roughly twenty-two gallons of water. Rice balls made with molasses and rock salt act must be provided as special treats at the end of each match. All games must end by noon to avoid the afternoon heat. The World Elephant Polo Association (WEPA) adheres to strict guidelines regarding the safety and well-being of the elephants. The tournament takes place every December in Chitwan National Park. It includes sixteen domesticated Asian elephants, half of them from Tiger Tops and the others brought in by other Nepal National Parks. The elephants are accompanied by their mahouts,

who usually have been partnered with the
animals for several years.

If you're not into elephant polo or cannot
be in Nepal at this time of year, elephant-back
safaris are offered in the parks. We participated
in elephant safaris while in Chitwan and it was a
fun and thrilling experience. So much better than
a jeep safari! And we got to bathe our safari
elephant in the river afterwards, which was also
a fun and thrilling experience.

http://www.elephantpolo.com/ and
http://www.tigertops.com/elephant-camp/

**FYI: Asia's seventy-million-year-old Himalaya
mountain range separates the Tibetan Plateau from
the Indian subcontinent and is spread across five
countries: Nepal, Bhutan, India, China, and Pakistan.
It is the youngest mountain range in the world. The
word "Himalaya" means "abode of snow" in
Sanskrit. The Himalayas are home to the god Shiva,
according to Hindu mythology.**

8. Take a mountain flight. Second only to
riding and bathing an elephant, was our Mt.
Everest Flight. It is exhilarating to fly over the
world's highest mountain peak and it was
amazing that we did it in a matter of minutes.
The pilots called us into the cockpit one by one
to see the peak up close and take photos, which
was pretty exciting. We were almost too close!
You fly out of Kathmandu airport early in the
morning for this hour-long air adventure. You
get to see much more than Everest, although that
is the highlight of the flight. Everyone has a
window seat, so the viewing is good for the
entire flight. On occasion, the flight has to be
cancelled due to weather, which changes fast in
this part of the world. You will receive a refund
or the option to take a later flight. For an
extreme adventure, you can charter a helicopter

and take a tour of the Everest valleys and fly into
the Everest range. The experience includes
landing in the valley and having breakfast before
returning to Kathmandu. Other options include
microlight flights to Annapurna and paramotor
flying. https://www.buddhaair.com/mountain-
flight-nepal/everest-experience.html and
https://www.viator.com/tours/Kathmandu/Flight
-Over-the-Himalayas-including-Mt-Everest-
from-Kathmandu/d5109-5588KTMFLIGHT and
http://www.everestflight.com/ and
https://www.yetiairlines.com/destination/everest
-express?dest=everest-express

**FYI: Many explorers and climbers were killed trying
to reach the summit of Everest before British
explorer Sir Edmund Hillary and his Sherpa guide,
Tenzing Norgay, were the first to reach the summit of
Mount Everest on May 29, 1953. Twenty five years
later, Reinhold Messner of Italy and Peter Habeler of
Austria were the first to reach the summit without
using supplemental oxygen! Nepal celebrates Mt.
Everest Day on May 29 every year in memory of the
first summit of Mt. Everest by Sir Edmund Hillary
and Tenzing Norgay Sherpa. The day is celebrated
with memorial events, processions, and special events
in Kathmandu and the Everest region.**

9. Skydiving over the Himalayas. If a
mountain flight is too mundane for your
adventurous spirit, step it up with Himalayas
skydiving. Nepal now offers skydiving options
with 360∘ view of the Himalayas. Emerging
as an extreme aerial adventure (no doubt!),
Everest skydiving is one of the most unique
experiences in the world. Skydiving is done
from a plane or a helicopter at the world's
highest drop zone a—Gorak Shep, Kala
Patthar. Your free fall is in front of some of the
world's highest mountain peaks, including
Everest. Experienced pilots with skydiving
ratings man the aircraft, but you should probably
worry more about your ripcord than your pilot.
Skydiving can be either a solo jump or in
tandem. https://www.everest-skydive.com/

FYI: The Himalayas are home to the highest lake on earth, Tilicho, and the deepest lake on earth, Shey Phoksundo. They are also home to some of the tallest mountains on earth, including Mount Everest.

10. Try meditation at Kopan Monastery.

Courses deal with Mind Training, Karma, Death and Dying, Bodhicitta, and more. There are 5-day and 10-day courses and even a month-long meditation course. Additionally, there are short courses on Tibetan medicine, Thangka painting, and the most popular is a ten-day course in Buddhist psychology and philosophy. Some students spend months at the monastery devoted to their studies. Young boys from many different Nepali ethnic groups come to the monastery to study to become monks. They receive a formal education in math, science and other subjects, as well as their spiritual studies.

It is the home of 360 monks, lamas, teachers and workers. The monks come from all Nepal and Tibet and range in age from 6-60-years old. Kopan Monastery was once open to visitors all week but were eventually overwhelmed with visitors, so entry has been restricted. There is a private road into the monastery, but it is a pleasant one-hour hike from Boudha. Having reached Kopan Monastery, you might as well visit the Phulhari Monastery, which sits on a hill higher than Kopan. In between Phulhari and Kapan is the

Vajrayan Monastery. Phulhari is worth a visit for the amazing Thangka paintings that adorn the entire I and the interiors of the halls. The building was designed by an American architect who combined the best of eastern and western architecture.

There are buses that go up to the base of the hill on top of which the Kopan Monastery is perched. Taxis can be hired too. Other alternatives are to hire a motorcycle or rent a mountain bike. During special pujas, large crowds of devotees climb up to the monastery to receive blessings and pay homage. A restaurant with great views of Kathmandu is open to the public and serves very good food.

http://www.kopanmonastery.com/

FYI: The people of Nepal greet each other with their palms placed together. They bow their foreheads and say "Namaste," which means, *"I salute the God in you."*

Nepalese Recipes

Get in the mood for your trip by making some classic Nepalese cuisine. Here are two traditional recipes.

Chicken Bhutua is a classic, spicy Nepalese dish

- 1 – 2 lb. Chicken – cut into small or medium pieces

- 5 minced garlic cloves

- minced ginger

- 3 minced red chilies

- 1 tbsp. cumin powder

- 1 tsp turmeric

- 1 tbsp. mustard oil

- 1 cup cut green onions

- 4 tbsp. mustard oil

- 1 tsp black pepper (ground)

- Half tsp cinnamon powder

- 5 whole cloves

- 1 tsp fenugreek

- Salt

Mix together the chicken, cumin, turmeric, salt, pepper
and 1 tbsp. mustard oil. Heat the 4 tbsp. mustard oil in a
pan. Place fenugreek in pan until dark. Then add cloves
to fry. Place chicken in pan and allow to brown. Next

add the chilies, ginger and garlic. Continue to stir-fry
chicken until completely cooked adding water if it
catches on. Now mix in onions and cinnamon, cooking
for a further 2 minutes. Serve with vegetables.

**Or if you are a vegetarian, try this Vegetarian Momo
recipe (makes 50)**

1 Tbsp. grated ginger

1 tsp turmeric

2-3 Tbsp. vegetable oil

5 cups diced cabbage, (about 1 small cabbage)

2 carrots, shredded (about 2 cups)

1/2 large onion, minced (about 1 cup)

salt & pepper, to taste

1 package Wonton wrappers, cut into circles

Grate/chop/shred vegetables. Cook the fresh ginger and
turmeric in oil for about a minute. Add onion and
cabbage. Season with salt and pepper. Cook until
softened and yellowish. Remove mixture from the heat.
Stir in the carrots. Set aside to cool.

How to fold the Momos:

Add a bit of water around the inside edge of the wrapper,
then add a small spoon of stuffing. To make the half-
moon shape you must use round wrappers. Cut them
with a cookie cutter before you stuff if they are square.
Use your fingers to pinch sides together to make a little
mountain ridge. Press that ridge down towards you,
crimping together the edge. Now create a second ridge
by pressing the top layer of dough together again. Fold it
over towards you and you will have two pretty mountain
ridges. The momos will naturally curve like the moon as
you go. Look at photos online (also on the next page) to
see how the momo should look. And don't worry, you
will get the hang of it after the first few.

Steam them in an oiled steamer (should be bamboo or
metal) until the dough is cooked thoroughly—about 25-
30 minutes. But depending on what wrappers you use,
cooking times will vary. Serve with condiments of your
choice, such as chili sauce, soy sauce, or sirracha.

Burfi

Delectable milk cakes for dessert or for a snack.

- 1 cup ricotta cheese
- Half cup ghee
- Half tsp cardamom powder
- 1 cup sugar

Combine ricotta, cardamom and sugar. Fry mixture in the ghee until golden brown or bake for 10 to 15 minutes in 300F oven. Pour onto a greased tray and cut into squares. Allow to cool.

FYI: Nepalese cuisine is more or less a hybrid of Indian, Thai, and Tibetan cuisines.   Some common dishes:

Momo (pictured here) is Tibetan-style dumplings with Nepalese spices. Momo is one of the most popular foods in Nepal. They are filled with goat meat or chicken or vegetables for vegetarians.

Chow Mein is a Nepali favorite based on Chinese-style stir fried noodles.

Dal-bhat-tarkari is the standard meal eaten
twice daily. It is a broth with lentils served over
rice or vegetables and is very spicy. There are
many variations of this dish.

Thukpa is a Nepalese hot noodle soup with meat
stock (yak, goat, lamb, and/or chicken) and
vegetables. This is often served with Momo.

Yogurt (*dahi*), potatoes, rice, curried meat
(*masu*), or fish (*machha*) are often served as side
dishes. Common ingredients in Nepalese cuisine
include tomatoes, cumin, coriander, chilies, peppers,
garlic and mustard oil.

Because of the cold temperature, people often
prefer hot foods, such as soup, ramen, and strong
tea or a strong fermented alcohol. A popular
beverage is butter tea, which is when salted
butter is added to tea. Milk or buttermilk and

sugar or the juice of sugarcane is usually added to tea. Nepal has rustic distilleries that make Raksi and millet beer.

Popular snack include dry-roasted soybeans, beaten rice (chiura), dried fruit candy (lapsi), and South Asian sweets. Western culture has influenced Nepal, especially in the way of food. Increasingly, pizza, burgers, soda, potato chips and biscuits (packaged cookies) are consumed.

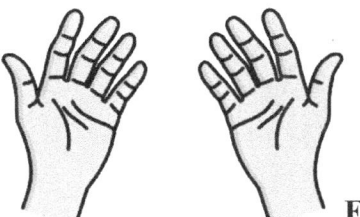 **FYI: Nepalese etiquette…Food is brought to the mouth with the fingers of the right hand. The left hand should never touch food, but may hold cups and glasses. The right hand should be rinsed before and after eating.**

TOURISTY THINGS TO SEE & DO

**Note: Kathmandu Valley has <u>130</u> historic
sites. You don't want to spend all your
precious time rushing from shrine to shrine.**

Instead, I recommend you visit the famous historical ones, which I have detailed. Use the rest of your time doing other cool stuff, such as an Everest Mountain Flight, trekking, a Chitwan safari, a Nepalese cooking class, try meditation or go to a yoga retreat—whatever interests you. But the important thing is to make the most out of your time at the "Rooftop of the World."

Boudhanath Stupa (God of Wisdom), circa 5th
century, is probably the most visited site in
Kathmandu. This is probably because it is
widely believed that whoever visits the stupa
with a pure heart received good karma and all
their wishes fulfilled. As if that's not enough, the
gates of hell are closed to them! It is certainly
the most widely recognized monument due to its
distinct features. It is also the largest in
Kathmandu and one of the largest in South Asia

at 118 feet (36 meters). Built circa 14th century, the monument was created after the passing of Buddha. It was built to be—and remains—a site of worship and prayer. On each side of the stupa are a pair of the all-seeing-eyes of the Buddha, which is meant to symbolize awareness. $.

https://www.facebook.com/Boudhanathstupa

FYI: Kathmandu's motto is 'Unity in Diversity'. That's good since there are more than five dozen different ethnic groups here!

Budhanilkantha Temple, also known as also known as the Narayanthan Temple, is dedicated to Lord Vishnu. The highlight of a visit to this shrine is the giant, horizontal statue of Lord Vishnu lying on a bed of black serpents in the middle of a pond. This is the largest stone carving in Nepal. According to legend, a farmer was working in his field one day when his plough struck a boulder. The farmer grew frightened when he saw blood seeping out of the stone. As he carefully dug out the big boulder, he discovered it was a statue, not a boulder.

City Museum is a one-of-a-kind museum and gallery housed in a new, modern building in the heart of the city. Free Wi-Fi, Coffee, light meals, and pastries are available in the café. If you're into art and photography or you have extra time, you should go. $. http://thecitymuseum.org/

Durbar Square is an ancient square in the middle of Kathmandu. It features exotic temples and palaces, including Taleju Temple (oldest), Shiva Temple, Narayan Temple, Vishnu Temple, Krishna Temple, Kumari Palace (home of the Living Goddess) and many more! There is a small admission fee to this UNESCO World

Heritage Site but it is well worth it and once
inside you may explore on your own. However,
there are lots of youths that hang out here in
hopes of being hired as a guide. Just say "No,
thank you." and keep moving and they will leave
you alone.

Freak Street. (Jhhonchen Tole or Jochen Tole).
Back in the early 1970s, this was the place for
hippies. There were New Age enlightenment

shops, cheap hostels, and a whole lot of hippies here. Since the era of flower power is gone, it no longer resembles its namesake. Nonetheless, some travelers find Thamel too touristy nowadays and prefer this area near Durbar Square. Also, you want to check it out because everything is cheaper here than in Thamel, including lodging, dining, and shopping.

FYI: The Kathmandu valley has three Durbar Squares; Kathmandu Durbar Square, Patan Durbar Square, and Bhaktapur Durbar square.

Garden of Dreams is a neo-classical historical garden and lovely spot to enjoy a little downtime. Located near the King's Palace, the garden dates back of the 20th century. It was a private garden belonging to a high-ranking Rana official. In addition to enjoying the serenity of the garden and its surrounding ponds, pergolas, pavilions, trellises, and amphitheater, there is a museum and plenty of space to take a rest or

read a book. Kaiser Café on site serves Nepalese
and Continental food: breakfast, lunch and
dinner. At one time, this was considered one of
the best private gardens. The center city oasis
was not opened to the public until 2007, but now
it is open to all from 9 a.m. – 10 p.m. My
favorite feature is the sunken flower garden. $.
http://gardenofdreams.org.np/

Narayanhiti Palace Museum is the former
royal palace (Narayanhiti Durbar), which served
as the primary residence for the country's
monarchs. It was built on the occasion of the
marriage of King Birenda Bir Bikram Shah, who
was next in line to the throne. The palace area
covers seventy-four acres and is fully secured
with walls and gates on all sides. The palace was
the scene of a terrible tragedy. On June 1, 2001,
King Birendra, Queen Aishwarya, and family

members were killed in a massacre. After the
massacre of King Birendra and his family, his
brother, Gyanendra, became the King of Nepal,
but his rule was short-lived. By 2008, Nepal
became a democratic republic. The king was
given fifteen days to vacate the throne and
palace. After that, the once private residence was
opened to the public as a tourist attraction. The
palace museum is closed on Tuesdays and
Wednesdays. $.

https://www.facebook.com/NarayanhitiPalaceM
useum/

National Museum, The. Religious, secular and
military artifacts of all kinds are housed in the
three buildings comprising this museum
complex. $. http://www.nationalmuseum.gov.np/

Natural History Museum. This museum showcases Nepal's natural history. I have not visited it, but I have read reviews and most who have visited suggested it was not worth your time. $. But if you have the time and an interest in natural history, you should go.
http://www.nhmnepal.edu.np/

Pashupatinath Temple (*See Terrance's Top Ten Picks*).

Swayambhunath Temple (*See Terrance's Top Ten Picks*).

Thamel is a commercial neighborhood in Kathmandu and it is also the best place for tourists. There is virtually nothing a tourist could want or need that cannot be found here, such as cheap lodging, handicrafts, restaurants, travel agencies, money exchange booths, pubs, clubs, mobile phone stores, food vendors and small grocery stores, clothing stores, and trekking gear. But be warned, the streets are narrow and bustling with activity. Pedestrians, cars, taxis, and rickshaws line these small streets and alleys. It is also the first place in Nepal to get Wi-Fi.

The Toothache Tree. If you work in the dental industry or are suffering from a toothache, you'll want to pay pilgrimage to the Toothache Tree. According to legend, a cutting from a special tree known as Bangemudha, the chunk of wood that has been put in place smack in the heart of Kathmandu's dental district, as a sort of wishing well. People with toothaches or other dental ailments visit the site and nail a coin to the tree as an offering to Vaishya Dev, the Newar God of the toothache. Supposedly there is a teeny tiny little idol inside of the main hole of the shrine, although the coins nailed on every part of the log obscure any view inside. In fact, the log is so covered that none of the actual wood is visible anymore either. Obviously, there are a lot of believers!

FYI: Nepal is the oldest country in South Asia. The average age of life expectancy is 59. Perhaps this is because more than twenty percent of kids ages 13-15 years old smoke. Or perhaps it is because the average spent on healthcare is $68pp annually. That is most likely because most people earn low wages.

Other cities that comprise Kathmandu Valley besides Kathmandu…

Bhaktapur is the third largest city in Nepal and makes up the three holy cities or kingdoms in the Kathmandu Valley. Located ten miles

outside of Kathmandu, the city was founded
during the 12th century AD by King Malla and
remains well-preserved. Because vehicles are
prohibited, it is a quieter place than Kathmandu,
which is about seven miles (12km) away. There
is a small admission fee to enter Bhaktapur
Durbar Square. There are many historic sites
here, including temples and the Palace of 55
Windows.

Patan. Across the Bagmati River from
Kathmandu is Patan, which is one of Nepal's
largest cities. You can explore Patan Durbar
Square, but most travelers go to shop. Patan is
famous for its metal and wood-carved
handicrafts and Thanka paintings. Many come
here to shop to avoid the chaos of Thamel.

FYI: To find out the exact fees for all heritage sites in Nepal and times of closures,

https://www.welcomenepal.com/plan-your-trip/heritage-site-entry-fees.html

Adventure

Adventure Activities

Just about any activity and type of tour is possible seasonally, such as paragliding, bungee jumping off Bhote Khosi Bridge (second highest bungee jump in the world), whitewater rafting on the Bhote Khosi River's Class 3-5 Rapids (or Trishuli and Seti for Class 2 & 3 Rapids), wildlife safaris, rock climbing, skydiving, kayaking, mountain biking, canyoning, mountain flights, zip flying, and trekking. Here are some useful resources.

http://nepalesetrekking.com/

http://www.taan.org.np/

http://www.nepaltrekkinginfo.com/index.html

http://www.kathmanduhotel-link.com/kathmandu-tours

https://www.bookmundi.com/kathmandu/d112-bm

https://nepaltraveladventure.com/nepal/adventures-in-nepal.php

http://adventuretravelnepal.com/

http://www.himalayansocialtravel.com/destination/destination_type/nepal

Nepal Association of Travel & Tour Agents (NATTA), www.natta.org.np

Nepal Association of Tour Operators (NATO), www.nepaltouroperators.org.np

Trekking Agencies' Association of Nepal (TAAN), www.taan.org.np

Society of Travel & Tour Operators – Nepal (SOTTO), www.sottonepal.org

**FYI: Mostly from the mountainous region of eastern
Nepal, Sherpas are an ethnic group often hired as
guides and porters for mountain expeditions. Not
only are they expert climbers, they don't suffer**

altitude sickness or other common climbing conditions because of genetics. Today it has become common to call all guides/porters 'Sherpas'.

Chandragiri Cable Car Ride. This is one of the newest activities offered in Kathmandu. The ride up the side of Chandragiri Hill rewards you with an impressive and unique view of the Himalayas. In ten minutes or so, you will complete a panoramic view of the Himalayas. Once you reach the top, you can stay as long as you like. There is a good restaurant—not to mention the view! When you are ready, you can descend and catch a final view of the Mighty Himalayas. http://chandragirihills.com/

Cultural Dinner Show. Enjoy an unforgettable dining experience with entertainment at Nepali

Chulo, one of Kathmandu's top-rated restaurants.
Amid the luxurious decor of this former palace,
indulge in a candlelit dinner — a seasonal, 4-
course meal featuring traditional Nepalese food.
Throughout the evening, watch a cultural show
that highlights the classic music, dancing and
costumes of Nepal. The food is good, but not
great. However, this three-hour event is more
about Nepalese culture (the show), than the
dinner. https://www.facebook.com/nepalichulo/

Kathmandu Countryside Bike Tour. Cycle
through the scenic countryside just outside
Kathmandu, You will explore charming
Nepalese villages and ride on scenic roadways
during this half-day, small-group mountain bike
excursion that includes lunch, guide, and bike.
https://www.viator.com/tours/Kathmandu/Kath

mandu-Countryside-Bike-Tour/d5109-5076NPUA

Mountaineering (mountain climbing). There are 326 mountain in Nepal open for mountaineering, but 103 have still not been ascended! You should know that this requires a minimum of one month and is expensive. Obviously, you need to be in peak physical condition and have experience mountaineering. http://www.nepalclimbing.com/

Nepalese cooking class. Take a cooking class in Kathmandu with an organization that works to improve the lives of marginalized local women. Learn about Nepalese cuisine, ingredients, greenhouse farming, and more. Help to prepare several delicious dishes, then sit down to enjoy the meal with your hosts.

https://www.viator.com/tours/Kathmandu/Half-Day-Traditional-Cooking-Class-in-Kathmandu/d5109-5060P28?pub=vcps

Orientation Sightseeing Tour. I like to do these on day one so that I quickly become familiar with a place. That way I know what I want to explore on my own and what is feasible to do timewise. I also get ideas for additional activities or learn what I should skip as not being worthwhile or what areas seem unsafe, etc. Here are links to see Kathmandu sightseeing/city tours:

https://www.viator.com/Nepal/d724-ttd

https://www.bookmundi.com/kathmandu/kathmandu-day-tour-4306?tp=1

https://www.bookmundi.com/kathmandu/kathmandu-valley-day-tour-3225?tp=1

https://www.bookmundi.com/kathmandu/sightseeing-day-tour-in-kathmandu-2775?tp=1

https://www.bookmundi.com/kathmandu/explore-kathmandu-city-4333?tp=1

Or go for a 2.5 hour **night tour** and see the city in a different light,
https://www.bookmundi.com/kathmandu/kathmandu-by-night-2250?tp=1

Spiritual adventure. Take a four-hour yoga class at a yoga center across from the holy Boudhanath Stupa. *"Our yoga teaching encompasses the Eight-Fold Path as taught by Lord Buddha while cultivating the Seven Disciplines. This totally holistic approach to life liberates both body and mind, creating a wellness that cannot be found in any other way.*

This is the spirituality of the Himalayas!" Full day and multi-day yoga retreats are also available.

https://www.viator.com/tours/Kathmandu/The-Boudhanath-Yoga-Experience-in-Nepal/d5109-64605P2

Whitewater rafting. Nepal has the most scenic and diverse white-water rafting or kayaking in the world. Whether you're a first timer or a pro or looking for a half-day or week-long expedition that includes camping and jungle treks, there is something for you with rapids ranging from 1 to 6. Plan your rafting trips with local operators, who have well trained river guides. You will find them in Kathmandu. Rivers open for rafting include Seti, Trishuli, Marshyangdi, Kali Gandhi, Karnali, Sunkoshi, and Tamur.

Here's a trip that I think would be a good option
for those with limited time:

Himalayan Whitewater Rafting Trip. The trip
departs at 6:30am from your hotel in
Kathmandu. Drive about 2.5 hours to reach the
rafting starting point Charaudi. After your
rafting preparation, orientation, and safety
instructions with a professional rafting guide,
begin your 3-hour stunning rafting experience
down the Trishuli River. Trishuli offers exciting
rapids and beautiful scenery. The outing ends
about 3pm at Kurintar, where you will then
enjoy lunch at a local restaurant. After lunch,
you will take the bus back to Kathmandu. Long
day (10 hours) but great price!

https://www.viator.com/tours/Kathmandu/Himalayan-
White-Water-Rafting-Day-Trip-from-
Kathmandu/d5109-36777P3

Wildlife Safari. I think "a must" is to participate in a wildlife safari at Chitwan National Park. There are many options and you can wait until you arrive in Kathmandu to choose one or you can use a tour operator to book one. Here is my suggestion for a very affordable all-inclusive 2-night, 3-day Chitwan Wildlife Safari. During your stay, you can take a jeep safari, jungle safari, canoe safari, see a Tharu village, and much more, depending on your interests.

https://www.viator.com/tours/Kathmandu/3-Day-All-Inclusive-Chitwan-Safari-Tour-from-Kathmandu/d5109-28592P10

Zip Flying. If you're up for it, you can experience the world's longest, steepest, and fastest zipline. This is referred to as extreme zipling or "zip flying" and it is the first of its kind in Asia.

http://highgroundnepal.com/zipflyer/

FYI: Here's a great video showing you what you can expect when zip flying in Nepal.

https://www.youtube.com/watch?v=MsOzAbUt8n8

Sherpa (Nepalese trekking guide)

About Trekking in Nepal…

Nepal is home to an extensive network of trails known as the Great Himalaya Trails. The great thing about trekking in Nepal is that you can do

a two-hour trek or one that lasts for several
weeks. It can be a fairly easy trek or a very
difficult one. It is up to you and the route you
choose! The trails are well maintained and well
posted. Rustic lodges (teahouses) are available
for brief stops or overnight stays. Most trails are
open year round, but here's what you need to
know:

**September and October has the best weather and
clearest views, but no tents are available at Everest
Base Camp because summit climbs can only be
achieved in late April and early May. So, April/May
is full of tents and climbers, but weather and views
are not as nice as September/October.**

You can take a self-guided trek (for now but the
government may make a guide compulsory for
safety reasons) or hire a guide/porter. Hiring a

porter means that you are providing income to a
Nepali family. Trekking is the main source of
income in much of Nepal. I have never been too
proud to hire a porter. It gives me a chance to
interact with a local and provides support I will
need at some point. The same is true for hiring a
guide. You probably don't need one for a two-
hour trek, but for an all-day or multi-day trek, I
highly advise hiring one. If something
unexpected comes up, such as an injury or a bad
storm, you will be very glad you did.

Permits are acquired in Kathmandu (see
'Documentation' section for more information).
These permits are checked along the trekking
route, so be sure you go where your permit gives
you permission to go.

The three most popular treks are
Annapurna, Langtang, and Everest. If you're

into nature, Annapurna is best. It is full of
diverse landscapes and lots of flora and fauna.
Depending on your circuit, the trek is 3-28 days.
Langtang requires 5-18 days to complete,
depending on the circuit. For sheer bragging
rights, trekkers choose Everest, which takes 6-30
days to complete. All three routes offer good
teahouses (lodges) along the way. I always think
of scones and fine china when I think of a
teahouse. But, of course, that is not what a
Nepalese teahouse is! Most trekkers in Nepal
make use of Nepal tea houses, which are small
hotels known (teahouse is "bhatti" in Nepali)
that offer a place to sleep and home-cooked
meals. The food is quite good and abundant. The
lodging ranges from rustic to very nice, but
don't expect anything luxurious, especially at
the higher altitudes. As you ascend, hot water

and showers become increasingly hard to find.
The good news is that teahouses are very cheap,
but there is an additional fee for charging
stations (for mobile devices) that can run about
the same cost as your room. Also, you will find
treats, such as chocolate and chips. But again,
the price increases as you climb higher. Also, be
sure to make reservations in high season as the
lodging becomes more limited as you climb
higher, which is why the price goes up. It's all
about supply and demand. If you don't have a
reserved bed, there may not be one available.

More tips: Hydrate. Hydrate. Hydrate.
Getting dehydrated will worsen altitude
sickness, cause diarrhea, and make the climb
much tougher in general. I like Boots brand of
sachets. https://www.boots.com/boots-
rehydration-treatment-6-sachets-10074961. Talk

to your doctor about a prescription for
Acetazolamide (Diamox) to treat altitude
sickness.

Add scented dryer sheets to your bag to
keep dirty clothes smelling nice and fresh.

Bring your own small pillow or at least a
pillow case. It is best not to trust the cleanliness
in a trekking teahouse. Bring a thin blanket or
cover sheet too (or lightweight sleeping bag), if
space permits. Bring some kind of shoes you can
wear in the shower and around the teahouse. Do
not go barefoot, even to the bathroom in the
middle of the night!

Speaking of the bathroom, bring small
packs of tissues to use as toilet paper. You will
find that some teahouses have none! Other
useful items include hand sanitizer, trail mix,
instant coffee, lemon ginger tea bags and coca

leaf tea bags (combats altitude sickness), and
non-chocolate protein bars so they won't melt.

Speaking of food, it is best to stick to rice
and bean dishes. Think vegetarian while on the
trek. Trust me!

Visit your local outfitter store and talk to
your trekking company, if you hired one, to find
out exactly what clothing and gear you need to
bring. Much of what you need can be purchased
in Nepal.

Here is a sample Everest Base Camp
itinerary:

Day 1: Fly from Kathmandu to Lukla
(strict flight weight of 33 pounds) and then trek
four hours to Phakding (where you will spend
the night. 8,500 feet elevation.

Day 2 & 3: Six-hour trek to Namche
Bazaar where you will spend night and next day

to acclimatize. 1,200 feet elevation.

Day 4: Six-hour trek to Tyangboche and
overnight.

Day 5: Six-hour trek to Dingboche and
spend the night. 14,000 feet elevation.

Day 6 & 7: Six-hour trek to Labuche and
overnight and next day to acclimatize. 16,000
feet elevation.

Day 8: 2.0-2.5 hour trek to Gorapshep and
spend the night. 17,000 feet elevation.

***Day 9: Final trek to Everest Base
Camp. Close to 18,000 feet elevation. Must also
hike back to Gorapshe for overnight.

Day 10: Six-hour trek to Pheriche.

Day 11: Four-hour trek to Tyangboche
and overnight.

Day 12: Five-hour trek to Namche Bazaar
and spend the night.

Day 13: Seven-hour trek to Lukla and overnight before flying back to Kathmandu the next day.

Even a trek to base camp shouldn't be attempted without a guide. A couple of good companies are **Trek Nepal Int'l**, https://treknepal.com/ and Exodus, http://exodustrekking.com/.

If you forgot to pack something or didn't want to try to get walking sticks through airport security, you can buy almost anything you need in Thamel or Namche Bazaar. Make sure you have local currency on the trail as exchange rates are unfavorable.

More resources can be found at:

https://www.atlasandboots.com/best-

mountaineering-books-ever-written/

**FYI: Lukla's Tenzing-Hillary Airport is maybe best
known for having being the world's most dangerous
airport. There no radar devices and the airstrip is on
a slope with a 3,000-meter drop into the valley on one
side and a steep cliff on the other. Each safe landing
is a heroic feat by the pilot. Weather conditions often
shut down the airport for hours or days. But to reach
Sagarmatha National Park and trek to Everest Base
Camp, this half-hour flight is the best way.**

There are two Everest Base Camps: South Base Camp and North Base Camp. The Everest South Base Camp trek on the south side is one of the most popular trekking routes in the Himalayas and is visited by thousands of trekkers each year. Trekkers usually fly from Kathmandu to Lukla, the "Gateway to Everest". If you wish to do the North Base Camp Trek you will have to get a permit from the Chinese government, plus a Tibet permit.

FYI: Earlier in this reference I mentioned that you can take a one-hour Mt. Everest Flight. You can also take a one-day Everest Base Camp Helicopter Tour, https://www.bookmundi.com/kathmandu/1-day-everest-base-camp-helicopter-tour-4335?tp=1.

Other trekking options include:

4-Day Kathmandu Valley Trekking Tour including Bhaktapur. Experience the heart of Nepal when trekking through the wilderness of Kathmandu Valley and staying overnight in small villages. Expect to stay in budget accommodations such as local teahouses, gaining insight into local culture along the way. Your expert guide can offer advice and help uncover the region's hidden gems. You'll have free time for optional activities, plus an array of food choices available in each town. Meals are not included, so you decide where and what to eat, with the flexibility to choose meals that suit your palate and budget.

https://www.viator.com/tours/Kathmandu/4-Day-Kathmandu-Valley-Trekking-Tour-Including-Bhaktapur/d5109-5912HNAK

FYI: The Yeti is said to live in the remote Himalayan region. This mysterious creature is akin to North America's Big Foot. Sir Edmund Hillary led a 1958 expedition to find the Yeti, but without success. Only about a dozen people have claimed to have seen the Yeti. Among those include the father of Tenzing Norge Sherpa, the first person to climb Everest. Like the father of Tenzing, most of the others who saw the Yeti felt sick and then died within a few days of seeing the Yeti. The creature has been seen in the

Khumbu region, which is at foothills of the Everest.
The Yeti diet is yaks, sheep, and other small animals.
Many people feel, however, that the Yeti is a peaceful
creature. In fact, known in Tibetan as
"Metohkangmi," the Tibetan believe that Yeti is the
protector of the doors to Shambala. In Tibetan
Buddhist and Hindu traditions, Shambhala (pictured
here) is a mythical kingdom hidden somewhere in
Inner Asia. No good photos have been taken during
these rare sightings, so this is more of an illustration
than a realistic depiction of the abominable
snowman. No good photos have been taken during
these rare sightings, so this is not necessarily a
realistic depiction of the abominable snowman.

BEST OF KATHMANDU

I've already addressed the best activities and
attractions, and in the next chapter I address the
best accommodations. Here are a few more
things you should know:

BEST SOUVENIRS: Nepal is known for wood
carvings (vases and boxes), stone carvings
(statues), singing bowls, Thangka paintings,
pashminas, rice paper items, carpets, gold and
silver or bead jewelry, Gurkha knives, Nepali
tea, prayer wheels, puppets, spices and
medicinal herbs (only buy these from a reputable
dealer), and traditional masks. Real antiques will
have a government certification, so be careful
you don't get scammed. Please note that
bargaining is normal in Nepal, so be prepared to
haggle with the seller.

BEST SHOPPING: For
cheap souvenirs, you can't beat **Thamel** and
Freak Street. For a higher quality of souvenirs,
go to **King's Way**, which is near Thamel. Please
note these are mostly brand name stores.
Another place to find name brands and more is
the mall. Considered to be the biggest mall in the
country, **City Mall** has a movie theater,
restaurants and food kiosks, shops, and
game/entertainment area.

FYI: A Singing Bowl may be one of the nicest souvenirs to take home. These metal bowls make a soothing sound when the rim is rubbed in a circular motion by a small wooden stick. Aside from the soothing sound, the vibration created by the bowl is said to be ideal for meditation ambience and has healing qualities. The singing bowl comes in various sizes, but there are only two types of singing bowls— machine-made or handmade. The handmade bowls are more basic in design but more expensive than machine-made, while machine-made bowls are perfectly symmetrical, highly decorated, and inexpensive.

BEST DESSERT: Sikarni is a dish made with yogurt and dry fruits. It is light and sweet—a perfect way to cap off your lunch or dinner.

BEST DINING: For fine dining, the options are limited in this backpacker's paradise. However, **Le Sherpa** does fine dining right and has a wine cellar.

BEST BEVERAGE: Nepal is a land of tea drinkers, so it is hard to find a good cup of coffee, but **Rosemary's Kitchen** is probably your best bet (www.rosemary-kitchen.net/). Nepalese tea is delicious and there are many varieties. **Rakshi** is the big liquor drink, but be warned that this distilled rice beverage is potent. If you like wine, **Tongba** is something interesting to try. Beer drinkers should drink

Everest Beer because the others have odd aftertaste or leave you with a heavy head in the morning.

FYI: A very interesting fact about the food habits of the Nepalese is that they avoid the use of metal spoons. Metal spoons are believed to detract from the flavor of food, so they use silver cutlery or their right hand to eat.

BEST SPA TREATMENT: Full Body Massage and Shirodhara, which is an Ayurvedic (Ayurveda) treatment using a warm blend of essential oils. Shirodhara soothes, energizes, nourishes, and relaxes the nervous system. It is good for chronic headaches, sleeplessness, anxiety, tension, and body/muscle pain—or for weary travelers!

https://www.viator.com/tours/Kathmandu/Himalayan-Herbs-Oil-Ayurveda-Treatments/d5109-8076P29/important-info

BEST NEPALESE FOOD: Bhojan Griha (and Kamasutra Bar). You will dine traditional style, which is on large, colorful cushions on the floor. Folk music and dancing often accompanies meals.

http://www.bhojangriha.com/.

FYI: Visitors should avoid drinking tap water and eating raw produce. Fruit that you peel and bottled water are safe. Do not eat around the temples or the monkeys will harass you.

BEST TIBETAN FOOD: Utse has provided exceptional Tibetan food for more than thirty years in Thamel. The best part is that the prices are very reasonable.
http://www.utsehotel.com/dinning.html

BEST BRUNCH: Moksh is one of the trendiest places in Kathmandu and serves a delicious (but not cheap) brunch.

BEST BAR: Sam's Bar in Thamel is a great place to relax at the end of a busy day of sightseeing. Be warned that it is tucked away so you'll have to ask for good directions.

BEST BAR FOR TREKKERS: Rum Doodles is a favorite and a rite of passage. Read stories of

other trekkers who have come before you. They
are posted all over the bar on huge cut-out
footprints!

BEST MOCKTAILS: Non-drinkers should
head to **Mezze**. They serve the best non-
alcoholic concoctions and wood-fired pizzas.

BEST NIGHTLIFE: Liquid Happiness. There
is music and a big variety of whiskey. I doubt
anywhere else in Kathmandu stocks so many
single malts.

BEST LOCAL AND INTERNATIONAL TOUR OPERATORS:

Boundless Journeys,
https://www.boundlessjourneys.com/asia/nepal/

Easy Tours,

https://www.easytours.travel/nepal.htm#group-tours

Intrepid Traveler,

https://www.intrepidtravel.com/us/nepal

Goway Travel,

https://www.goway.com/trips/dest/asia/cntry/nepal/

Himalayan Experience,

http://www.himalayanasiatours.com.au/

Mountain Sherpa Trekking & Adventures,

http://www.nepaltrekkingtours.com/tour/nepal-tour.html

REI Adventures,

https://www.rei.com/adventures/trips/hiking#

Sherpa Tours, http://www.sherpatours.com.au/

G Adventures,

https://www.gadventures.com/trips/nepal-himalaya-highlights/ANENG/

Gecko Adventures,

https://www.geckosadventures.com/en-us/search?country=Nepal

Explore, https://www.explore.co.uk

Tucan Travel, https://www.tucantravel.com/

ABOUT ACCOMMODATIONS

Rentals

There are a surprising number of options given the relatively small size of Kathmandu, including houses, guesthouses, and apartment rentals. To find a **vacation rental**, I recommend using www.airbnb.com, www.trivago.com, and www.booking.com. Search "Kathmandu" to find all listings. I found listings on Airbnb as low as $10 for a room in an apartment or as low as $20 to rent the entire apartment in peak season—and the rooms and apartments looked quite nice. I found a double room for $13 a night in a B&B and a double room for $37 a night in a four-star boutique hotel. Both options included breakfast, no cancellation fee, and no prepayment needed. Another option is to find lodging upon arrival, which is easy to do as there are signs posted everywhere. Also, other travelers are more than happy to let you know where they are staying or about a good place they have heard about in Kathmandu. Here are some more options.

Budget Travelers:

BEST BUDGET HOTEL: Hotel Mustang Holiday Inn. Located in Jyathal/Thamel, it's hard to beat all this hotel has to offer for the price and great reviews. I found a rate on hotels.com of $14 for one room for two adults in peak season. Amenities include free internet, gift shop, bar, laundry service, tour desk, restaurant, safe, room service, doctor/nurse on call, security guard, mail service, housekeeping, room service, bar, and transfers. Plus, they have a back-up power generator, which is good in a city with planned power outages.

CHEAPEST HOTEL: Hotel Red Panda has rooms as low as $5 a night. It doesn't get any cheaper than this! Plus, is in clean, located in Thamel, there is a small restaurant and 24-hour room service. http://hotelredpanda.com/

For more budget traveler options:

http://www.kathmanduhotel-link.com/kathmandu-accommodation-budget

http://www.kathmanduhotel-link.com/kathmandu-accommodation-midrange

Backpackers:

BEST BACKPACKER LODGING: Thamel Backpackers Home is in the middle of the action in Kathmandu and offers 24-hour Wi-Fi, single rooms to family apartment, library, dining hall, laundry services, in-room tea/coffee service, private bath with hot showers, rooftop restaurant,

television, personal safe, multi-lingual staff, and
more. Book online and receive a 15% discount.
Free cancellation. Single rooms start at $12 in
peak season and a double room at $15.
http://www.thamelbackpackers.com/

For more Backpacker options:

http://www.kathmanduhotel-link.com/hotel-
type/kathmandu-backpackers

Hotels:

**BEST BOUTIQUE HOTEL: Aspara Boutique
Hotel** is the best place for those looking to
splurge. It features a lovely restaurant, hot
breakfast served in a big breakfast room, large
lobby, and deluxe guest rooms with sitting areas
and satellite television for less than $100 a night
in peak season. http://apsaraboutiquehotel.com/

BEST LUXURY HOTEL: Hotel Yak & Yeti

Hotel Yak and Yeti. This is a luxury five-star hotel in the heart of Kathmandu, Nepal. The hotel was once a palace, but has been renovated to provide modern conveniences, such as a lobby bar, shopping arcade, atrium, jogging track, a swimming pool and two tennis courts, Café Restaurant, and brand new Club Nirvana Fitness Center complete with state-of-the-art gymnasium and Nirvana Spa. Hotel Yak & Yeti has a comprehensive Business Centre and is the first hotel in Kathmandu offering a an exclusive Executive floor and Club Shangri-La. Facilities on this floor include 24-hour butler service, a private lounge for breakfast and cocktails, a boardroom, and in-room outlets for fax machines and computers, which can be rented.

https://www.yakandyeti.com/

Guesthouses:

BEST GUESTHOUSE: Shree Tibet Family Guesthouse Established since 1992 and run by a Tibetan Family, the staff is super helpful and friendly. They will assist you with travel plans (including trekking) and answer questions about local attractions and activities. Rates are reasonable and include Wi-Fi. Their location in Thamel can't be beat. Airport pickup, laundry service, and storage are available. Travelers may start their day with coffee on the rooftop (which boasts a rooftop garden). They serve Nepali, Indian, Chinese and continental food from the hotel restaurant, which has inside and roof top seating. The views of the Himalayas, Swayambhunath Monkey Temple, and Kathmandu can be viewed from their rooftop (pictured here). http://www.hotelshreetibet.com/

For more guesthouse options:

http://www.kathmanduhotel-link.com/hotel-type/kathmandu-guesthouses

 **FYI: There are three things that differentiate a guest house or B&B from a hotel. Number one is the size. They are usually much smaller than hotels, so they usually have less amenities, a smaller staff, and fewer guests. Guesthouses and B&B's are family businesses, unlike hotels that are typically owned by corporations. Lastly, Guesthouses and B&B's are not as strictly regulated as hotels. This means they may not be as clean or maintained as well. On the other hand, many owners take great deal in providing the best possible service to their guests. They are able to provide more "homey" touches. Reviews on places such as *TripAdvisor* and *Trivago* are the best way to make sure you find one of the best guest houses or B&Bs, as well as for hotels and other rentals.**

Hostels:

As to be expected, there are lots of hostels here and they vary greatly. Hostels began as cheap lodging for backpackers and students. However, they have changed a great deal over the years. While some remain "clean but basic," others are better than four star hotels! The trick is to find the right hostel. Word of mouth from other travelers is the best way.

Hostelworld is another good resource. **Hostelworld: Hostels & Cheap Motels Travel App** is available for free at https://itunes.apple.com/app/hostelworld.com/id3488908 20.

You can also get this travel app at:

https://play.google.com/store/apps/details?id=com.hostel
world.app&referrer=mat_click_id%3Dc46797768025dc
874d86662df367c410-20180307-8816

BEST OVERALL HOSTEL: Alobar1000.

This hostel offers free blankets and linens
(including duvets!), free Internet, library, free
city maps, free satellite television, rooftop
movies, hot showers, and a friendly staff.
Airport pick up and drop off service is available.
One free activity is offered every night on the
rooftop, such as a Nepali culture class, game
night, trekking class, and night city tour.
Alobar1000 encourages interaction with fellow
travelers and is happy to store luggage and assist
with travel plans. Be advised that taxi drivers
will tell you that this hostel is full when it is not,

so asked to be dropped off anyway.

http://alobar1000.wixsite.com/alobar1000

BEST HOSTEL FOR SOLO TRAVELERS: Zostel Kathmandu. This is a multi-story hostel located in Thamel. Options range from eight bed dorms to private rooms. There is a rooftop bar, garden café, free Wi-Fi, book exchange, free linen, 24/7 reception, and game room, which includes Baagh Chaal, a traditional Nepalese game. Zostel is very popular with American, British, and Australian travelers.

https://www.zostel.com/zostel/Kathmandu/

BEST BUDGET HOSTEL: Wander Thirst Backpacker Hostel. This hostel offers lots of organized activities, such as yoga classes, Meditation, Game, Dance, Bon-Fire, and Camping nights, Hikes, Biking Tours and more.

Furthermore, they have hot showers, free linen, free city maps, high speed Wi-Fi, bicycle/motorbike/car rentals, taxi service, restaurant, travel assistance, dance floor, social room, and accessible rooftop with a great view of Kathmandu. Credit cards not accepted.

http://www.hostelwanderthirst.com/

BEST HOSTEL FOR COUPLES: Hotel Ganesh Himal. Private rooms are available and cost as little as $29. This serene hostel was established in 1977, so it has served thousands of travelers. They have recently completed renovations that include an expansion. They now offer both budget ($20 night) rooms and deluxe rooms ($120) with discounts available on the deluxe rooms when you book online. I love their cozy lobby and outside sitting areas.

http://www.hotelganeshhimal.com/

**BEST PARTY HOSTEL: Monkey Temple
Hostel Kathmandu.** 24-hour reception, free
linen, free Wi-Fi, hot showers, luggage storage,
book exchange and board games. Dorm rooms
and private rooms are available. Weary travelers
will appreciate their two-storied rooftop
restaurant and bar overlooking Swayambhunath
Monkey Temple. One-day cancellation policy.
https://www.hostelworld.com/hosteldetails.php/
Monkey-Temple-Backpackers-
Hostel/Kathmandu/272407

BEST B & B: Zen Bed and Breakfast. Located
in Thamel, Zen provides budget dorms and
private rooms. There is a small restaurant that
serves home-cooked meals, rooftop terrace,
travel desk, free Wi-Fi, money exchange, wake
up calls, luggage storage, and 24/7 reception.
https://www.hostelworld.com/hosteldetails.php/
Zen-Bed-and-Breakfast/Kathmandu/87619

Outside Kathmandu…

BEST LODGE IN CHITWAN: Eden Jungle Resort. Their restaurant serves Nepali, Indian, and Western dishes made with ingredients from their organic garden. Eden Jungle Resort is in Sauraha Village located nearby the government elephant stable and the national park entrance. The resort is built in Chitwan's typical style, equipped with all the modern comforts, including 24-hour hot water. The surrounding area is full of shaded gardens. Canoe safaris, jungle safaris, elephant back safaris, a visit to the elephant breeding center, and cultural show are available. http://www.edenresort.com.np/

BEST LODGE IN CHITWAN: *It's a tie!* **Tiger Tops Elephant Camp is as good as Eden Jungle Resort**. Located on the edge of Chitwan National Park, Tiger Tops Elephant Camp offers you up-close time with their twelve Asian elephants. The camp consists of six safari tents with attached bathrooms (toilets and hot showers) and electricity. There is a lovely dining hall, free Wi-Fi, and charging station. Many different activities and packages are available. http://tigertopselephantcamp.com/portfolio/the-camp

Pokhara

BEST ACCOMMODATIONS IN

POKHARA: If you venture over to **Pokhara**,
the best place to stay is **Pokhara Eco-Lodge**.

Very good prices, centrally-located, and eco-friendly. http://www.pokharaecoresort.com/

Mum's Garden Resort is also a good place to stay in Pokhara.
http://www.mumsgardenresort.com/. Pokhara is a trekking gateway to the Annapurna. This lakeside community offers spectacular scenery and lots of adventure activities.

If you're looking for something different…

Himalayan International Yoga Academy. Forget city life for a while and try one or more of the special packages offered at Himalayan International Yoga Academy (HIYA). This facility is set amongst about

30,000 sq. ft. of land in a pristine hilly location south of the city. It has a bungalow named *Kailash* and four tented camps called *Wisdom, Tranquility, Harmony* and *Bliss*. Organic foods are grown and served. The Yogic and Naturopathic specialists promise to rejuvenate your body, mind and soul. Services include *Yoga, Meditation, Spa, Pancha-Karma, Ayurvedic Clinic* and other customized packages. Yoga lessons are available, as well as Alternative/Ayurvedic Medicine, outdoor spa facilities, cooking courses, massages, cycling, and educational experiences.

http://www.kathmanduhotel-link.com/Himalayan_International_Yoga_Academy

FYI: Public displays of affection are frowned upon in Nepal.

If you are invited into a Nepali home, remove your shoes before entering. Be sure to be invited inside before entering.

At dinner time, you must wash your hands and mouth prior to eating.

Always wait for the host to serve you.

ABOUT NEPAL

The early history of Nepal is largely unknown. It is believed that the Kiratis arrived during the 7th or 8th century. The Kathmandu Valley was divided up into several self-governed areas that were somewhat united as one larger kingdom.

Little is known about the Kirata, except they include Lord Shiva, Lord Buddha and Valmiki. From about 400 AD, the Kirata Empire collapsed and was replaced by the Liccahavi Dynasty, which was later replaced by the Malla Dynasty and then the Shah Dynasty. It was 2008 before Nepal abolished the monarchy and became the Federal Democratic Republic of Nepal. This makes Nepal the youngest republic in the world.

The president of Nepal serves as chief of state, while the prime minister is head of government. A Cabinet or Council of Ministers fills out the executive branch. Today, Nepal has a unicameral legislature with the Constituent Assembly totaling 601 seats: 240 members are elected, 335 seats are awarded by proportional representation, and 26 are appointed by the

Cabinet. The Sarbochha Adala (Supreme Court) is the highest court.

While there are five dozen different ethnic groups in Nepal with the main ones being Chhettri, Brahman-Hill, Magar, Tharu, Tamang, Newar, Muslim, Kami and Yadav, most of the people are Hindu. Buddhism only accounts for about twelve percent. However, these numbers are deceptive as many Nepalese people practice a combination of Hindu and Buddhism. Many holy sites are shared between the two faiths, which also worship some of the same gods. The rest of the population practice Islam, Kirat Mundhum, or Christianity.

There are more than 100 recognized languages. The most commonly spoken languages are Nepali, which is spoken by nearly 60 percent of the population, and Nepal Bhasa

(*Newari*). Other common languages in Nepal
include Bhasa, Maithili, Bhojpuri, Tharu,
Gurung, Tamang, Awadhi, Kiranti, Magar, and
Sherpa.

As a result of its many years of isolation,
Nepal is one of the least developed nations in the
world. Despite its energy-production potential,
Nepal remains one of the world's poorest
countries. One of the reasons for its slow
development is its energy issues. People have to
consistently endure up to twelve hours a day
without electricity due to an overwhelming
demand.

Nearly eighty percent of the country is
mountainous. The Great Himalaya Range,
ranging in elevation from 14,000 to nearly
30,000 feet, contains the world's highest peaks.
These include Everest, Lhotse, Makalu, Cho

Oyu, Dhaulagiri, Manaslu, Kachenjunga, and
Annapurna. Except for a few tiny villages or
settlements, this area is uninhabited. Luckily for
Nepal, the world wants to see and/or climb some
of these mountains. Nepal has opened 326 peaks
for mountaineering and climbing expeditions.
Much of the country's revenue is generated by
trekking permits and tourism spending. While
the rest of the world calls Mt. Everest
'Sagarmatha', the Nepalese Sherpas call it
'Chomolungma', which means "Goddess
Mother of the World."

While the capital city of Kathmandu has
the largest population, there are four other major
cities in Nepal, including Pokhara, Patan,
Biratnagar, and Bhaktapur.

Key dates in history include the Treaty

with Britain affirms Nepal's sovereignty (1923),
Nepali National Congress created (1947), First
constitution of Nepal introduced by Prime
Minister Padma Shamsher Rana (1948), Nepal
and the United Stated establish diplomatic
relations (1948), Sir Edmund Hillary and
Tenzing Norgay become the first climbers to
reach the top of Mount Everest (1953), Nepal
joined the U.N. (1955), multi-party constitution
adopted (1959), Crown Prince Dipendra kills
King Birendra (2001), The government signs the
Comprehensive Peace Agreement (CPA) ending
the decade-long insurgency with the Maoists
(2006), the monarchy was dissolved and Ram
Baran Yadav becomes Nepal's first president (
2008), Sixteen Nepalese Sherpa guides die in an
avalanche on Mount Everest in the worst
recorded accident in the mountain's history

(2014), Nepal and India sign a deal to build a $1bn hydropower plant on Nepal's Arun river to counter crippling energy shortages (2014), A 7.8-magnitude earthquake strikes Kathmandu and its surrounding areas killing more than 8,000 people, causing mass devastation and leaving millions homeless (2015), and China and Nepal hold their first ever joint military exercise (2017).

FYI: Thousands of Nepalese citizens fought as British soldiers during World Wars I and II. There are still as many as 5,000 Nepalese Gurkhas serving in the British Army. For a more in depth study of Nepal's history, the best book to read is *A History of Nepal* by John Whelpton.

This is a typical tea stall for trekkers.

ANNUAL EVENTS & AVERAGE TEMPS

Festivals and Events

Nepal probably has more public holidays and festivals than anywhere else in the world. But it can be problematic to find out exact times, dates, and locations for these events. That's because the Nepali New Year is based on the Hindu calendar which is set about 57 years ahead of the Gregorian calendar. Please note that some businesses and tourist sites may close, depending on the festival. Also, the streets may be very crowded, depending on the festival. It may be difficult to get around or you may become claustrophobic! Here is the best resource for getting accurate, up-to-date information, http://www.calendar-nepali.com/festivals.html

Because there are so many festivals, I have
included only the biggest:

Losar (Tibetan New Year); a three-day
celebration

Shivaratri (celebration of Lord Shiva)

Holi (Festival of Colors)

Bisket Jatra / Navavarsha (Nepali New Year)

Buddha Jayanti (Buddha's Birthday)

Ropain (Rice planting festival)

Janai Purnima (Sacred Thread Festival)

Gai Jatra (Festival of Cows)

Teej (Festival of Women)

Yenya (Indra Jatra & Kumari Jatra) Kathmandu
Festival

Ganesh Chaturthi (celebration of Hindu God Ganesh)

Dashain

Tihar/Newari New Year (Festival of Light)

Chhath Parva (celebration of the Sun God Surya)

Christmas (more for tourists than locals and mostly decorations not a festival)

New Year's Eve and Day (again more for tourists than locals and celebrations mostly confined to Thamel and Pokhara)

FYI: The main Nepalese festivals that travelers to usually enjoy are Shivaratri, Holi, Tihar and Losar.

This is one of the nicer tea houses for trekkers.

Average Temps

Summer in Nepal

June to mid-September is summertime and
monsoon season, and the daily forecast typically
consists of extremely high temperatures and high
probability of rainfall. Eighty percent of all the
rain in Nepal is received during the monsoon
(June-September).

Fall in Nepal

From late September to November are dry with
pleasant temperatures. This time of the year is
considered the best to go trekking in the
Himalayas thanks to the fresh air and clear skies.

Winter in Nepal

December to February tend to be mild in the
daytime but very cold at night, especially in the

mountains. While winter is okay for trekking, January is the coldest month of the year and many mountain lodges shut down due to the extremely low temperatures.

Spring in Nepal

March to May offer pleasant temperatures and sporadic rain. Next to fall, spring is considered the best time to go trekking. Flowers begin to bloom during this time and it is easy to spot wildlife.

 **FYI: Interestingly, it rarely snows in Kathmandu. You have to go to higher elevations to see snowfall.**

June is the hottest month in Kathmandu with an average temperature of 73°F (23°C).

The coldest month is January at 49°F (9°C).

April offers the most daily sunshine hours a day—12!

The wettest month is July with an average of 13" (325mm) of rain.

<u>Averages</u>

Spring=60-73°F (15-23°C)

Summer=75-78°F (22-25°C)

Autumn=60-75°F (15-25°C)

Winter=48-53°F (8-12°)

To see the most current weather forecast,

https://www.worldweatheronline.com/kathmandu-weather-averages/np.aspx

FYI: Touching anything with your feet is considered offensive in Nepal. The head is considered to be the most sacred part of the body, so don't touch someone's head, even if you're just playing around.

Some handy phrases...

Hello – *Namaste*

My Name Is.. – *Mero Naam ... Ho*

Goodnight – *Subha ratri*

Cheers! (Used when drinking or as a greeting) – *Subhakamana!*

How much Is This? – *Yo kati ho*

Thank You – *Dhanyabad*

Stop! – *Rokinuhos*

Where is the toilet – *Shauchalaya kata cha? (Sa-u-chha-la-ya ka-ta cha?)*

I'm Lost – *Ma haraye*

Take me there, please – *Kri-payaa, ma-lie tya-haa, laa-noos*

Best Currency Conversion: www.oanda.com

Best App for Organizing Travel Documents:
https://www.tripit.com

Best Language Translator: *Google Translator
(Apple & Google Play Store)*

Best City Maps: *CityMaps2Go* (Apple Store)

**FYI: Lumbini, Nepal is the birthplace of
Buddha.**

How to Pack

Nepal is a conservative place, so you should
dress conservatively. You can wear t-shirts, but
they shouldn't be sleeveless. Your legs should
be covered for the most part (knees should not
be seen), so it is best to wear long pants, Capri
pants, cargo shorts (if extend past knee), or long
skirts—definitely no short shorts, mini dresses,
or short skirts. What you pack depends on what
season you go to Nepal and what activities you
plan to do. You will pack differently if going
trekking than sightseeing, or according to the
season.

If traveling in the winter or trekking, bring an all-weather (waterproof) coat, hat, scarf, gloves, good quality socks, sweaters, and all-weather hiking boots. Be sure to also bring good walking shoes and/or some kind of comfortable shoe to wear inside the tea house/lodge. If you buy new boots for your trip, be sure to break them in well before leaving home. The same is true for your backpack. If you buy a new pack for your trip, be sure to stuff it full and walk around with it to get used to carrying a load before you leave home. Trust me when I tell you that even a modest backpack can feel heavy after a few hours.

Bring yummy, healthy snacks that won't melt or take up much room, such as protein bars and trail mix.

In summer, always carry a lightweight, water-resistant jacket. No matter what the season, be sure to bring at least 30 SPF sunscreen and lip balm.

Pocket-size eye drops are a good idea, especially if you wear contacts, due to the high altitude and high probability of dry eye.

If trekking, bring a lightweight towel, hand sanitizer, and handy wipes to use when you can't wash your hands or when a shower is not an option. See 'Trekking' for more packing tips.

Bring a reusable water bottle.

Head lamp (optional but advisable) for trekkers or flashlight/mini-lantern. Electricity is limited throughout Nepal, remember? The same is true for toilet paper. Buy a couple of rolls in Kathmandu and put in your backpack. It gets scarcer and more expensive the higher up the trail you go.

Dress in layers. Dress in layers. Dress in layers. *Got it?*

Be sure to bring water shoes, bathing suit, and dry wick shirt and pants if going rafting.

Pack more socks than you normally do as they get dirty and stinky fast on this kind of trip (especially trekking) and you can't hand wash and dry thick socks very quickly.

Bring a universal plug and voltage adapter kit for your electronics. Nepal uses 220V.

If you're going to be camping or renting a property, make sure to find out if you need to bring or rent towels, sleeping bags, linen, blankets, etc. If you need a sleeping bag, it is best to buy in Kathmandu rather than try to pack one. Be sure to buy a bag that will keep you warm in low temperatures.

I carry large plastic zip top bags so I can store wet bathing suits or dirty shoes. Also, I can safely store snacks and my important documents in these clear, plastic bags so I can easily find what I need in a hurry.

If you wear glasses, bring a spare pair. If you take medication, bring enough to last three or four days longer than your trip, in case you get delayed.

Be sure to pack a first aid kit. You can buy one or assemble your own.

Be sure to have some Nepalese rupee notes on you, especially if trekking. This is very important!

Battery life is shortened by cold weather so be sure to take that into account if you will be trekking. Trekkers usually put their batteries in their sleeping bags with them overnight. Also, be sure to have charging equipment for your batteries and mobile devices, as well as SIM cards, film, lenses, filters, or whatever you need for your equipment.

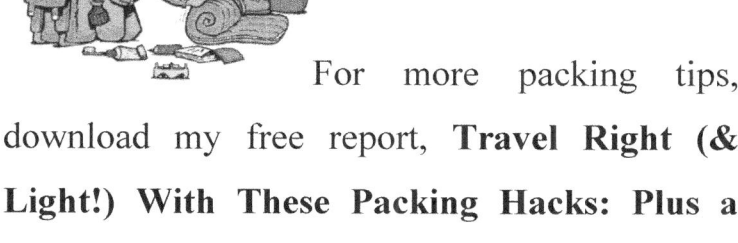 For more packing tips, download my free report, **Travel Right (& Light!) With These Packing Hacks: Plus a Packing   Checklist.** https://terrancezepke.com/product/travel-right-light-packing-hacks-plus-packing-checklist/

TERRANCE ZEPKE

Series List

Most Haunted Series

Terrance Talks Travel Series

Cheap Travel Series

Spookiest Series

Stop Talking Series

Carolinas for Kids Series

Ghosts of the Carolinas Series

Books & Guides for the Carolinas Series

& More Books by Terrance Zepke

≈

Terrance Zepke studied Journalism at the University of Tennessee and later received a Master's degree in Mass Communications from the University of South Carolina. She studied parapsychology at the renowned Rhine Research Center.

Zepke spends much of her time happily traveling around the world but always returns home to the Carolinas where she lives part-time in both states. She has written hundreds of articles and more than fifty books. She is the host of *Terrance Talks Travel: Über Adventures*. Additionally, this award-winning and best-selling author has been featured in many publications and programs, such as NPR, CNN, *The Washington Post,* Associated Press, Travel with Rick Steves, Around the World, *Publishers Weekly,* World Travel & Dining with Pierre Wolfe, *San Francisco Chronicle*, Good Morning Show, *Detroit Free Press*, The Learning Channel, and The Travel Channel.

When she's not investigating haunted places, searching for pirate treasure, or climbing lighthouses, she is most likely packing for her next adventure to some far flung place, such as Reykjavik or Kwazulu Natal. Some of her favorite adventures include piranha fishing on the Amazon, shark cage diving in South Africa, hiking Peru's Inca Trail, camping in the Himalayas, dog-sledding in the Arctic Circle, and a gorilla safari in the Congo.

Sign up for weekly email notifications of the **Terrance Talks Travel** blog to be the first to learn about new episodes of her travel podcast, learn cheap travel tips, access dozens of free downloadable TRAVEL REPORTS, and discover her TRIP PICK OF THE WEEK at www.terrancetalkstravel.com or sign up for her **Mostly Ghostly** blog and check out her GHOST TOWN at www.terrancezepke.com.

MOST HAUNTED SERIES

*A Ghost Hunter's Guide to the Most Haunted Places in
America* (2012)
*A Ghost Hunter's Guide to the Most Haunted Houses in
America* (2013)
*A Ghost Hunter's Guide to the Most Haunted Hotels &
Inns in America* (2014)
*A Ghost Hunter's Guide to the Most Haunted Historic
Sites in America* (2016)
*The Ghost Hunter's MOST HAUNTED Box Set (3 in 1):
Discover America's Most Haunted Destinations* (2016)

MOST HAUNTED and SPOOKIEST Sampler Box Set: Featuring
*A GHOST HUNTER'S GUIDE TO THE MOST HAUNTED PLACES
IN AMERICA* and *SPOOKIEST CEMETERIES* (2017)

*A Ghost Hunter's Guide to the Most Haunted Places in the
World* (2018)

≈

SPOOKIEST SERIES

Spookiest Lighthouses (2013)
Spookiest Battlefields (2015)
Spookiest Cemeteries (2016)
Spookiest Objects (2017) *Spookiest Box Set (3 in 1):
Discover America's Most Haunted Destinations* (2016)

≈

TERRANCE TALKS TRAVEL SERIES

Terrance Talks Travel: A Pocket Guide to South Africa (2015)
Terrance Talks Travel: A Pocket Guide to African Safaris (2015)
Terrance Talks Travel: A Pocket Guide to Adventure Travel (2015)
Terrance Talks Travel: A Pocket Guide to Florida Keys (including Key West & The Everglades) (2016)
Terrance Talks Travel: The Quirky Tourist Guide to Key West (2017)
Terrance Talks Travel: The Quirky Tourist Guide to Cape Town (2017)
Terrance Talks Travel: The Quirky Tourist Guide to Reykjavik (2017)
Terrance Talks Travel: The Quirky Tourist Guide to Charleston, South Carolina (2017)
Terrance Talks Travel: The Quirky Tourist Guide to Ushuaia (2017)
Terrance Talks Travel: The Quirky Tourist Guide to Antarctica (2017) *Terrance Talks Travel: The Quirky Tourist Guide to Machu Picchu & Cuzco (Peru)* 2017

African Safari Box Set: Featuring TERRANCE TALKS TRAVEL: *A Pocket Guide to South Africa* and *TERRANCE TALKS TRAVEL: A Pocket Guide to African Safaris* (2017)

Terrance Talks Travel: A Pocket Guide to East Africa's Uganda and Rwanda (2018)

Terrance Talks Travel: The Quirky Tourist Guide to Kathmandu (Nepal) & The Himalayas (2018)
Terrance Talks Travel: The Quirky Tourist Guide to Edinburgh (Scotland) (2018)

≈

CHEAP TRAVEL SERIES

How to Cruise Cheap! (2017)

How to Fly Cheap! (2017)

How to Travel Cheap! (2017)

How to Travel FREE or Get Paid to Travel (2017)

CHEAP TRAVEL SERIES (4 IN 1) BOX SET (2017)

≈

STOP TALKING SERIES
Stop Talking & Start Writing Your Book (2015)
Stop Talking & Start Publishing Your Book (2015)
Stop Talking & Start Selling Your Book (2015)
Stop Talking & Start Writing Your Book Series (3 in 1) Box Set (2016)

INDEX

F

festivals, 154
Freak Street, 82, 115

G

Garden of Dreams, 84
Great Himalaya Trails, 103

H

Himalayan International Yoga Academy, 143
Hostels, 133
Hostelworld, 133

K

Kaligandaki, 41
Kathmandu Valley, 8, 18, 35, 39, 43, 53, 75, 89, 90, 110,
147
Kopan Monastery, 64
Kumari. *See* Living Goddess

L

Living Goddess, 45, 81
Lukla, 30, 107, 109

M

Mount Everest. *See* Mt. Everest
Mount Everest Base Camp, 28
Mt. Everest, 7, 27, 36, 59, 61, 96, 110, 150

Made in United States
North Haven, CT
23 May 2023